MAD
SCIENTISTS

THE NOT-SO-CRAZY WORK OF AMAZING SCIENTISTS

BY SALLY LEE

CONSULTANT:
MICHAEL D. BENTLEY, PHD
PROFESSOR, DEPARTMENT OF BIOLOGICAL SCIENCES
MINNESOTA STATE UNIVERSITY, MANKATO

CAPSTONE PRESS
a capstone imprint

Fact Finders Books are published by Capstone Press,
1710 Roe Crest Drive, North Mankato, Minnesota 56003
www.capstonepub.com

Library of Congress Cataloging-in-Publication Data
Lee, Sally,
Mad scientists : the not-so-crazy work of amazing scientists / by Sally Lee.
pages cm.—(Fact finders. Scary science)
Summary: "Describes several scientists who went outside the box to discover scientific answers"—Provided by
publisher.
Includes bibliographical references and index.
ISBN 978-1-4765-3928-7 (library binding)—ISBN 978-1-4765-5126-5 (paperback.)—ISBN 978-1-4765-5975-9
(ebook pdf)
1. Scientists—Juvenile literature. 2. Scientists—Biography—Juvenile literature. 3. Discoveries in science—
Juvenile literature. I. Title.
Q141.L465 2014
509.2'2—dc23   2013032179

Editorial Credits
Jennifer Besel, editor; Veronica Scott, designer; Marcie Spence, media researcher;
     Jennifer Walker, production specialist

Printed in the United States of America in Stevens Point, Wisconsin.
092013   007769WZS14

TABLE OF CONTENTS

CHAPTER 1

DARING, BRAVE, AND A BIT ODD

Throughout history real scientists have done some strange experiments. They've eaten vomit. They've let snakes bite them. They've zapped dead bodies with electricity. And they've done it all in the name of science.

These daring scientists have all been called "mad scientists." But these people were not crazy or evil at all. Instead they were dedicated, smart scientists.

These scientists used methods that were unlike those used by others. They put themselves in harm's way—often unknowingly—to find solutions. They used unusual methods to answer questions.

Their stories are exciting and maybe a bit scary. But these brave scientists made some incredible discoveries. And those discoveries changed the way people live.

CHAPTER 2

STRANGE EXPERIMENTS

Giovanni Aldini stood over the dead body lying on the table. He touched the dead man's face with a charged rod attached to a strong battery. The man's eye opened and stared at Aldini. Then Aldini used a charged rod to make the man's legs kick and back arch. Horrified, people ran from the room.

Aldini wasn't a circus performer. He was a scientist in the early 1800s. Aldini was showing what electric currents did to a body. Through his experiments he proved that electricity runs from a person's brain to his or her muscles.

Aldini went on to use electric currents to treat people with mental illnesses. Zapping brains with electricity sounds dangerous—and it is. But in some cases, it's effective too. Doctors still use Aldini's electric ideas to treat some problems of the brain.

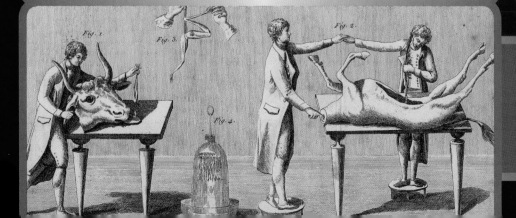

ALDINI ALSO USED ELECTRIC CURRENTS ON ANIMALS TO UNDERSTAND HOW ELECTRICITY AFFECTS BODIES.

ANOTHER SHOCKING DISCOVERY

About 100 years after Aldini, another scientist took the use of electricity to the next level. In the early 1900s, Dr. Louise Robinovitch thought that electric shocks could restart the hearts of people who died suddenly. Many people thought her idea was crazy. But that crazy idea turned out to be groundbreaking.

At first Robinovitch experimented with animals. She used electric currents to jump-start lab animals' hearts. When those trials worked, she tried the experiment on a woman who had died suddenly. Robinovitch placed electrical wires on the woman's chest and back. Then she switched the electricity on and off using the same rhythm as a beating heart. Soon the woman's heart was beating normally.

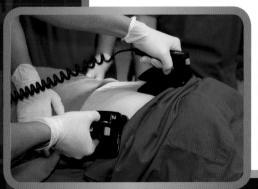

Robinovitch designed a machine that could deliver electric currents to patients in an emergency. Today we call this machine a **defibrillator**. Doctors use a modern version of Robinovitch's device every day, saving thousands of lives.

current—the flow of electrons
defibrillator—an electronic device that applies an electric shock to restart the heart

THE LIVING DOG'S HEAD

A dog's head sat on the table. But its body was no where to be seen. Yet the dog was able to stick out its tongue and lick its nose.

Sergei S. Brukhonenko created this bodyless dog. But he didn't do it for fun. He was a scientist looking for answers. In the late 1920s, Brukhonenko was a Russian heart surgeon. Back then, it wasn't possible to stop a heart long enough to repair it. Surgeons needed a way to keep blood moving through a body when the heart wasn't working.

Brukhonenko invented a machine called the autojector. This device had two pumps, some tubes, and a bowl of blood with added oxygen. One pump pushed the blood from the bowl into the dog's head. The other pump moved the blood out of the head and back to the bowl. The constant supply of oxygen kept the dog's brain alive.

Brukhonenko's autojector was the first machine that could keep a patient alive without a beating heart. His machine led to today's heart-lung machines that are still used during heart surgeries.

BRUKHONENKO WITH HIS HEART-LUNG MACHINE IN 1954

DISGUSTING DRINKS

Stubbins Ffirth collected the vomit of a yellow fever patient. He put it in a glass and drank it.

Why would anyone do something so gross? Ffirth was a medical student in the early 1800s. At that time some U.S. cities were dealing with outbreaks of yellow fever. It was a scary disease. In the worse cases, patients' skin turned yellow and blood turned their vomit black.

Ffirth noticed that outbreaks of the disease came during hot months. He came to believe that people didn't catch yellow fever from other people. A **contagious** disease would spread in any weather. Ffirth did some disgusting stuff to prove his idea. He not only drank vomit, but he rubbed it into cuts on his arm. He dribbled it into his eyes and sniffed the fumes of cooked vomit. But he never got sick. He proved that yellow fever wasn't passed from person to person.

A DEADLY EXPERIMENT

Ffirth proved that yellow fever wasn't contagious. But he didn't find out how yellow fever actually spread. Credit for that discovery goes to another mad scientist—Jesse Lazear.

Lazear was part of a team of doctors sent to Cuba in 1900. The team's goal was to find a way to stop the spread of yellow fever. Lazear had read studies by other scientists that said mosquitoes spread the disease. He believed those studies were right. To prove it Lazear secretly let a mosquito bite a yellow fever patient. Then he let the same mosquito bite him. Lazear was dead 12 days later.

Lazear left behind notes about his deadly experiment. Today mosquito control and vaccines have wiped out the disease in most countries.

contagious—easy to catch or spread
vaccine—a medicine that prevents a disease

A BACTERIA SMOOTHIE

Dr. Barry Marshall had seen ulcer patients suffer with pain for years. Ulcers are sores that form on the lining of a person's stomach, intestine, or esophagus. Before the 1980s, doctors believed that stress or bad diets caused ulcers. The only treatment they offered patients was to surgically cut out the sores.

But Marshall didn't think stress or food caused ulcers. His research had convinced him that bacteria were to blame. And if bacteria were the problem, antibiotics—not surgeries—were the answer. But other doctors didn't believe him.

Marshall felt he had to do an experiment to prove his idea. So one day in 1984, Marshall mixed bacteria from an ulcer patient's intestine with some broth and drank it. Five days later he woke up vomiting. His stomach hurt, and his breath smelled awful. Tests proved that the bacteria had given him the beginning stages of an ulcer. He then took an antibiotic, and the problem cleared up.

bacteria—one-celled, microscopic living things; many bacteria are useful, but some cause disease

antibiotic—a drug that kills bacteria

It took more than 10 years for doctors to believe Marshall's discovery. But once they understood his research, ulcer treatment changed forever.

FACT:

MARSHALL TRIED TO EXPERIMENT WITH LAB MICE. BUT MICE CAN'T GET ULCERS, SO HIS TRIALS FAILED. HE DIDN'T HAVE PERMISSION TO EXPERIMENT ON PATIENTS. THAT'S WHY HE EXPERIMENTED ON HIMSELF.

CHAPTER 4

DANGEROUS SITUATIONS

John Scott Haldane could barely breathe. He vomited and his head ached. Then he turned blue and passed out. Finally, a helper rescued him.

Haldane had shut himself inside a wooden box for nearly eight hours with no fresh air. This risky experiment had a purpose. Haldane was testing the effects of gases on the human body. He learned that too much carbon dioxide built up inside the box, making it impossible to breathe. This information could help workers on submarines breathe easier.

Haldane was a scientist in the early 1900s. He sniffed a lot of awful air to see how gases affected people. His studies of carbon monoxide gas saved the most lives. Haldane did 13 experiments in which he breathed in carbon monoxide. Carbon monoxide often built up inside mines after fires and blasting. Miners couldn't see or smell the gas. But breathing it was deadly. Haldane's work helped mining companies develop ways to keep workers safer.

carbon dioxide—a gas that people and animals breathe out
carbon monoxide—a poisonous gas produced by the engines of vehicles

HALDANE EXPERIMENTED WITH BREATHING MACHINES IN MINES AND OTHER SITUATIONS.

FACT:

WHEN DIVERS COME TO THE SURFACE TOO QUICKLY, GAS BUBBLES FORM IN THEIR BLOOD. THESE GAS BUBBLES CAUSE PAIN AND SOMETIMES DEATH. HALDANE FOUND THAT DIVERS COULD AVOID "THE BENDS" BY COMING TO THE SURFACE SLOWLY.

Painful burns covered Marie Curie's fingers. Her skin was cracked and scarred. She was weak and felt ill. But she blamed her problems on hard work, not on her famous discovery.

Curie and her husband, Pierre, were scientists in the late 1800s. They were researching the rays created by the element uranium. They found that one mineral gave off more **radioactivity** than they thought it should. Further study led them to two huge discoveries. They found that two new elements were causing the high radioactivity levels. They named these two new elements polonium and radium.

radioactivity—a process in which atoms break apart and create a lot of energy

Curie studied radium for years. Stories say she often carried some in her pockets. Pierre showed that radium could damage living tissue. This discovery led people to find ways to use radium to treat cancer—a treatment that is still used today.

But being in contact with radium for long periods of time is also very dangerous. At the time Curie didn't think that radium could kill her. But scientists now know that Curie died from a blood disease caused by too much radiation.

TOO MUCH OF A GOOD THING

Much like Marie Curie, Elizabeth Fleischman Ascheim ignored the warning signs that her work was hurting her. In the late 1800s, Ascheim became possibly the first person to open her own X-ray lab in California. She took X-ray pictures of soldiers during the Spanish-American War (1898). Later dentists sent patients to her to have teeth X-rays taken.

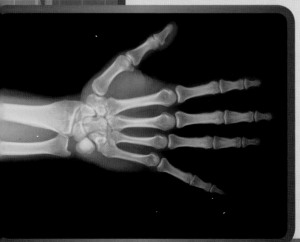

Ascheim never wore gloves or avoided the radiation given off by the X-rays. Over time the skin on her hands became hard and cracked. Ascheim blamed it on the chemicals she used. But the oozing sores and warts got worse. Doctors cut off her arm. But the radiation had caused cancer to rage in her body, and doctors couldn't save her.

HUMAN CRASH DUMMY

This was the most dangerous ride of John Paul Stapp's life. Helpers strapped Stapp into his seat on a rocket powered sled. A warning siren wailed. Then the sled's nine rockets blasted off, shooting fire behind them. The sled shot down the track toward the pool of water that would stop it. The sled—with Stapp on it—reached 632 miles (1,017 kilometers) per hour in only five seconds. Moments later, the sled hit the pool and slammed to a stop in just 1.4 seconds. The sudden stop was like a speeding car hitting a wall. The tiny blood vessels in Stapp's eyes burst. He was blind and in pain. Luckily, his vision returned the next day.

Stapp was a U.S. Air Force doctor. This record-breaking ride wasn't for fun. And it wasn't the only ride he took. Stapp was studying how many g-forces, or Gs, pilots could take. A "G" is the force of gravity you feel while standing on the ground. You feel more Gs when you quickly speed up, change direction, or stop. They're what you feel on roller coaster rides.

Scientists used to think people could handle up to 18 Gs. Stapp proved that was wrong. During his ride in 1954, he hit a record breaking 46.2 Gs.

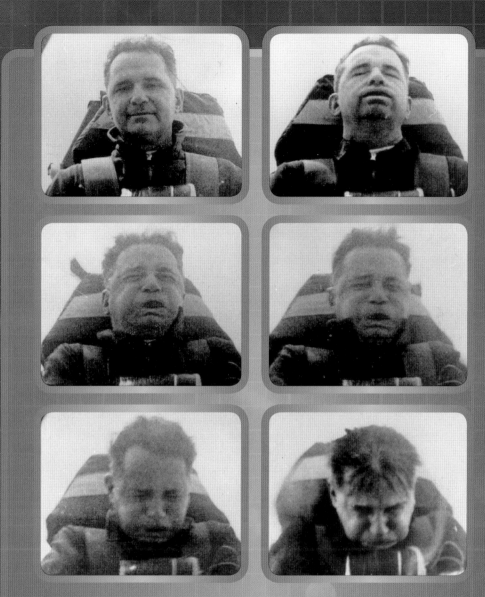

A CAMERA ON THE SLED CAPTURED PHOTOS OF JOHN PAUL STAPP DURING HIS RECORD-BREAKING RIDE.

FACT:

THE U.S. AIR FORCE BUILDS AIRPLANES STRONG ENOUGH TO WITHSTAND HIGHER GS BECAUSE OF STAPP'S CRAZY EXPERIMENTS.

CHAPTER 5

SELF SURGERY

Pain from a swollen appendix stabbed Dr. Evan O'Neill Kane's side. Kane knew how to remove it. He had done this type of surgery on others before. But that day in 1921, he needed the surgery himself. And he decided to try a new idea he'd been working on.

In the early 1920s, surgeons used general anesthetics to put a patient's whole body to sleep. Kane thought using a local anesthetic would be safer for patients. A local anesthetic would deaden only the area being operated on. But he hadn't been able to try the idea on anybody.

Kane propped himself up with pillows. A nurse held his head up so he could see the mirror above him. He deadened the area, and then cut into his side. When he reached the appendix, he pulled it up and snipped it off. The local anesthetic worked. Kane's surgery was practically painless. He even recovered faster than normal. Today, doctors and dentists use local anesthetics every day.

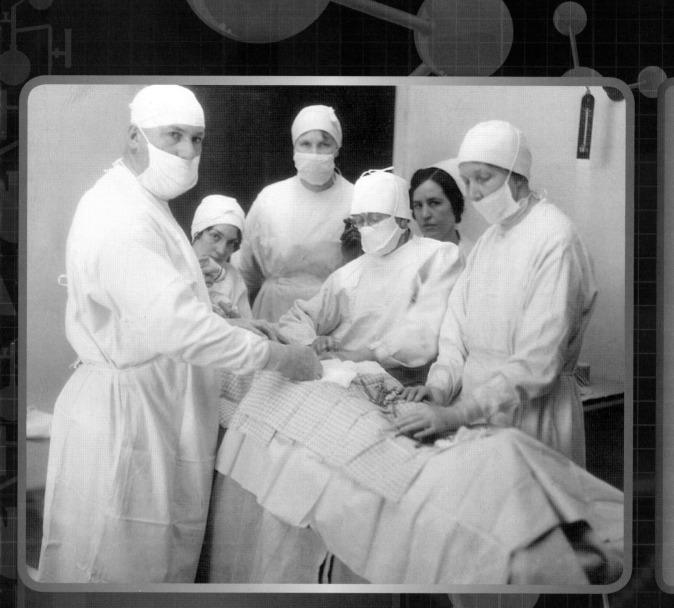

KANE (SECOND FROM RIGHT) PERFORMED A TOTAL OF THREE SURGERIES ON HIMSELF. THIS PHOTO FROM 1932 SHOWS KANE DOING SURGERY ON A PATIENT JUST TWO DAYS AFTER HE OPERATED ON HIMSELF TO CORRECT A HERNIA.

appendix—a small, closed tube attached to the large intestine

anesthetic—a substance that reduces sensitivity to pain

AIMING STRAIGHT FOR THE HEART

Every person Werner Forssmann asked said no. Everyone thought the medical student's idea was crazy. They said pushing a long, narrow tube called a catheter through his veins and into his heart was way too dangerous. They said his plan was crazy. But Forssmann didn't think his plan was crazy. A catheter would let doctors put medicine directly into the heart.

So one day in 1929, Forssmann did his experiment anyway. He pushed a hollow needle into a vein in his arm. Then he eased the catheter through the needle, into his arm, and toward his heart. Then he walked up two flights of stairs to have an X-ray taken. The catheter had slid into his heart without damaging his veins. His experiment was a success.

Forssmann was thrilled, but other doctors still thought he was crazy. He lost his job and had to stop working on the heart catheter. But two other surgeons continued Forssmann's research. Twelve years later, heart catheters were finally used on patients. They have been saving lives ever since.

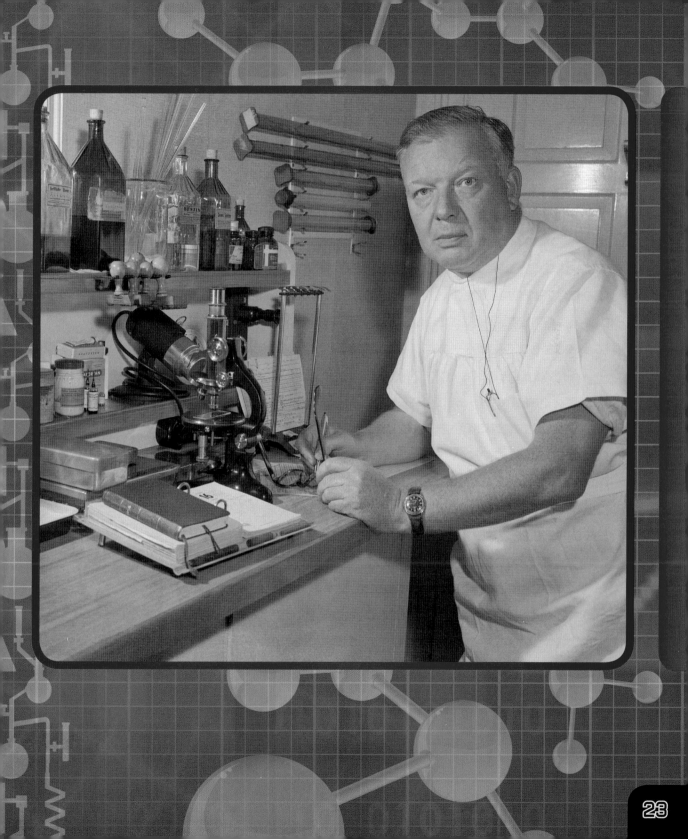

LIVING CYBORG

The surgeon cut into Kevin Warwick's arm. Then he put in a chip with 100 **electrodes** and attached the chip to Warwick's nerves. Thin wires poked out of Warwick's skin and connected to a control pad. Warwick knew the surgery was risky. One mistake could mess up his nerves or damage his brain. But he was willing to risk it to become a cyborg—part human and part machine.

Warwick is a scientist and college teacher. In 2002 Warwick, with the help of about 20 other scientists, plugged his nervous system into the Internet. This connection allowed Warwick to control machines with his mind. He could make an electric wheelchair move using only his thoughts. While he was in New York, his device sent signals through the Internet. It let him control a robotic arm in England.

Warwick's cyborg experiment lasted three months. But his test showed how these devices might one day help people with disabilities.

electrode—a point where an electric current can flow into or out of

FACT:

WARWICK'S WIFE, IRENA, ALSO HAD ELECTRODES PUT IN HER BODY. THE TWO COULD SEND SIGNALS TO EACH OTHER WITHOUT TALKING. WHEN IRENA CLOSED HER HAND, WARWICK COULD FEEL IT.

Tim Friede pulled a 12-foot (4-m) long black mamba from its cage. One bite from this deadly snake can kill a person within 20 minutes. Friede held the snake's head near his arm. The mamba struck, plunging its fangs into Friede. Blood dripping from the site showed that venom had reached his vein. Yet all Friede got was a swollen arm and hand.

Snakebites kill at least 100,000 people in the world each year. Medicine called antivenins could save most of those lives. But most of the deaths happen in the world's poorest nations. The people there can't get these drugs. Friede is proving that it's possible to build up immunity to snake venom. He hopes this will lead to a vaccine that would protect the people most at risk.

Friede had to train his body to deal with the poison. In 2000 Friede started giving himself shots of small doses of venom. Over time he increased the amount of venom he gave himself. Now he can survive bites that would kill anyone else.

immunity—the ability of the body to resist a poison or disease

CHAPTER 6

GROUNDBREAKING CRAZINESS

The scientists in this book, and many others, have done a lot of dangerous and disgusting things to reach their goals. For that, many people called them mad. But these scientists made many important discoveries.

It is important to remember, though, that the risks these scientists took were led by years of research and preparation. They did not do these experiments lightly. Some broke safety rules and were punished for it. And many died because of their work. Today, scientists must follow strict rules when doing experiments. Those rules are important for the safety of scientists and for any of their patients.

Many of today's technologies came from the work of scientists who did the unthinkable. Who knows what today's "mad" scientists might discover.

GLOSSARY

anesthetic (an-iss-THET-ik)—a substance that reduces sensitivity to pain, sometimes with loss of consciousness

antibiotic (an-ti-bye-OT-ik)—a drug that kills bacteria and is used to cure infections and disease

appendix (uh-PEN-dix)—a small, closed tube attached to the large intestine

bacteria (bak-TEER-ee-uh)—one-celled, microscopic living things; many bacteria are useful, but some cause disease

carbon dioxide (KAHR-buhn dy-AHK-syd)—a colorless, odorless gas that people and animals breathe out

carbon monoxide (KAHR-buhn muh-NAHK-syd)—a poisonous gas produced by the engines of vehicles

contagious (kun-TAY-juss)—easy to catch or spread

current (KUHR-uhnt)—the flow of electrons

defibrillator (de-FIB-yoo-lay-tur)—an electronic device that applies an electric shock to restart the heart

electrode (e-LEK-trode)—a point where an electric current can flow into or out of

immunity (i-MYOON-uh-tee)—the ability of the body to resist a poison or disease

radioactivity (ray-dee-oh-ak-TIV-uh-tee)—a process in which atoms break apart and create a lot of energy

vaccine (vak-SEEN)—a medicine that prevents a disease

READ MORE

Biskup, Agnieszka. *The Amazing Work of Scientists with Max Axiom, Super Scientist.* Graphic Science and Engineering in Action. North Mankato, Minn.: Capstone Press, 2013.

Krull, Kathleen. *Lives of the Scientists: Experiments, Explosions (and What the Neighbors Thought).* Boston: Houghton Mifflin Harcourt, 2013.

Royston, Angela. *Heroes of Medicine and Their Discoveries.* Crabtree Connections. New York: Crabtree Pub. Co., 2011.

INTERNET SITES

FactHound offers a safe, fun way to find Internet sites related to this book. All of the sites on FactHound have been researched by our staff.

Here's all you do:

Visit *www.facthound.com*

Type in this code: 9781476539287

INDEX